Potterdrunk

Magical Drink and Dessert Recipes
Inspired by The Wizarding World of
Harry Potter

BY

Thomas Beard

xxxxxxxxxxxxxxxxxxxxxxxxxxxxxxxxxxxxxxxxxxx

Table of Contents

Recipe 1 - Voldemort Cocktail................................ 5

Recipe 2 - Butterbeer....................................... 7

Recipe 3 - Witches Brew.................................... 9

Recipe 4 - The Harry Potter 11

Recipe 5 - Pumpkin Juice................................ 13

Recipe 6 - Golden Snitch Cake Pops 15

Recipe 7 - The Hufflepuff House 18

Recipe 8 - Butterbeer Hot Chocolate 20

Recipe 9 - The Ravenclaw House 23

Recipe 10 - Knickerbocker Glory 25

Recipe 11 - The Slytherin House 27

Recipe 12 - Bertie Bott's Jelly Beans................... 29

Recipe 13 - Gryffindor House......................... 32

Recipe 14 - Unicorn Blood Cocktail 34

Recipe 15 - Butterbeer Ice Cream 36

Recipe 16 - Polyjuice Potion 39

Recipe 17 - Avada Tequila 41

Recipe 18 - Goblet of Fire 43

Recipe 19 - Confunda Chambardo 45

Recipe 20 - The Albus Dumbledore 47

Recipe 21 - Chocolate Frog Jelly Shots 49

Recipe 22 - Firewhiskey 52

Recipe 23 - Butterbeer Jelly Shots 54

Recipe 24 - Pureblood 56

Recipe 25 - Pumkintini 58

Recipe 26 - The Phoenix Feather 60

Recipe 27 - Polyjuice Potion Jelly Shots 62

Recipe 28 - Liquid Luck 64

Recipe 29 - The Severus Snape 66

Recipe 30 - Amortentia – The Love Potion 68

Recipe 1 - Voldemort Cocktail

This cocktail is dark and dangerous much like its name sake Voldemort!

Serving Size: 1

Preparation Time: 15 minutes

List of Ingredients:

- Black Sambuca (1 cup)
- Absinthe (1/2 cup)
- Gin (1/4 cup)
- Lemon Zest (1/2 tsp)
- Lemon Bitters (1/2 tsp)
- Dry Ice (1 tablespoon)

xxxxxxxxxxxxxxxxxxxxxxxxxxxxxxxxxxxxxxxxxx

Instructions:

1. Add your first 5 ingredients with ice in a shaker.

2. Shake well and pour into a cold cocktail glass.

3. Add in your dry ice and serve.

xxxxxxxxxxxxxxxxxxxxxxxxxxxxxxxxxxxxxxxxxx

Recipe 2 - Butterbeer

Butterbeer, in the Harry Potter books, is painted to us as a foaming mug of slightly alcoholic liquid that is not so sickly butterscotch. Now we can create a pretty close replica using this recipe.

Serving Size: 1

Preparation Time: 10 minutes

List of Ingredients:

- Pumpkin Ale/Beer (12 fluid ounces)
- Butterscotch Sauce (5 tablespoons)

xxxxxxxxxxxxxxxxxxxxxxxxxxxxxxxxxxxxxxxxx

Instructions:

1. Add your beer to your blender and start running the blender on medium speed.

2. Slowly add in your butterscotch sauce in a steady stream while the blender continues to blend.

3. Continue to blend until just combined.

4. Serve and enjoy!

xxxxxxxxxxxxxxxxxxxxxxxxxxxxxxxxxxxxxxxxx

Recipe 3 - Witches Brew

A drink fits perfectly for a magical woman.

Serving Size: 1

Preparation Time: 10 minutes

List of Ingredients:

- Orange Juice (1/2 cup)
- Pomegranate Juice (1/2 cup)
- Vodka (1/4 cup)

xxxxxxxxxxxxxxxxxxxxxxxxxxxxxxxxxxxxxxxxxxx

Instructions:

1. In a large bowl, mix together all your ingredients and stir to combine.

2. Serve chilled and enjoy!

xxxxxxxxxxxxxxxxxxxxxxxxxxxxxxxxxxxxxxxxxxx

Recipe 4 - The Harry Potter

This delicious cocktail will have you casting spells like Harry Potter.

Serving Size: 1

Preparation Time: 15min

List of Ingredients:

- Vodka (1 oz.)
- Lemonade (1 cup)
- Blue Curacao (1 oz.)
- Dry Ice (1 teaspoon)
- Blue Sugar (2 tablespoons)

xxxxxxxxxxxxxxxxxxxxxxxxxxxxxxxxxxxxxxxxxx

Instructions:

1. Rim a cocktail glass in blue sugar.

2. Add your first 3 ingredients into a shaker with ice.

3. Shake well and pour into a cocktail glass.

4. Add dry ice and serve.

xxxxxxxxxxxxxxxxxxxxxxxxxxxxxxxxxxxxxxxxxx

Recipe 5 - Pumpkin Juice

It can be said that wizards used Pumpkin Juice to stay on top of their game.

Serving Size: 2

Preparation Time: 10 min

List of Ingredients:

- Pumpkin (1/2, seeded and cleaned, diced)
- Red Apple (1, cored and diced)
- Lemon (1, diced)
- Ginger (1 slice, peeled)

xxxxxxxxxxxxxxxxxxxxxxxxxxxxxxxxxxxxxxxxx

Instructions:

1. Add all ingredients to a juicer and extract the juices.

2. Strain the juices and discard the solid remains.

3. Serve over ice.

xxxxxxxxxxxxxxxxxxxxxxxxxxxxxxxxxxxxxxxxx

Recipe 6 - Golden Snitch Cake Pops

Now we can create our own Golden Snitch just like the one used in Harry's Quidditch games.

Serving Size: 6

Preparation Time: 40 minutes

List of Ingredients:

- Cake crumbs (1 cup)
- Cream Cheese (1/2 cup)
- White Fondant (1/2 cup, rolled)
- Golden Sprinkles (1 cup, edible)
- Yellow Candy (1/2 cup melted)
- Frosting (1 cup)
- Lollipop sticks (6)

xxxxxxxxxxxxxxxxxxxxxxxxxxxxxxxxxxxxxxxxxx

Instructions:

1. In a large bowl combine your cake crumbs and cream cheese together and knead slightly to form a pliable dough.

2. Once the mixture is manageable, start forming small balls from your cake dough then insert a lollipop stick into each ball.

3. Dip each ball into your frosting, layer on a clean cookie sheet and set in the freezer to harden for about 15 minutes.

4. Next set your melted yellow candy and golden sprinkles next to each other in separate bowls.

5. Dip your frozen cake balls first into the yellow candy then immediately roll into the golden sprinkle, and finally back to the cookie sheet.

6. Once all 6 have been coated, rest the balls in the refrigerator and start working on your fondant wings.

7. Proceed to cut 12 wings from your sheet of fondant and stick them into both sides of your cake balls (2 in each).

8. Keep refrigerated until ready to serve.

xxxxxxxxxxxxxxxxxxxxxxxxxxxxxxxxxxxxxxxx

Recipe 7 - The Hufflepuff House

Here we have the Hufflepuff house welcome drink.

Serving Size: 1

Preparation Time: 10 minutes

List of Ingredients:

- Pineapple Juice (1 oz.)
- Orange Juice (1 oz.)
- Rum (1 oz.)
- Ginger Ale (1 oz.)
- Schnapps (3/4 oz.)

xxxxxxxxxxxxxxxxxxxxxxxxxxxxxxxxxxxxxxxxxx

Instructions:

1. Add all your ingredients to a tumbler with ice.

2. Serve and enjoy!

xxxxxxxxxxxxxxxxxxxxxxxxxxxxxxxxxxxxxxxxxx

Recipe 8 - Butterbeer Hot Chocolate

All this sugar is bound to make you feel as if you are flying!

Serving Size: 4

Preparation Time: 15 min

List of Ingredients:

Topping

- Heavy Cream (1 cup)
- Sugar (3 tablespoons)
- Vanilla (1 teaspoon)
- Butterscotch sweets (10, small, to imitate butter drops on top)

Drink

- Milk (3 cups)
- Heavy Cream (1 cup)
- Butterscotch Chips (3/4 cup)
- Butterscotch Sauce (1/4 cup)
- Cocoa Powder (3 tablespoons)
- Vanilla (1 tsp)

xxxxxxxxxxxxxxxxxxxxxxxxxxxxxxxxxxxxxxxxxx

Instructions:

1. Set your milk to warm in a saucepan over medium heat. Once warm add all the remaining drink ingredients and stir to combine. Remove from heat and set aside.

2. Add the first 3 topping ingredients to a stand mixer and run until the cream becomes stiff.

3. Pour your hot chocolate ¾ way up in your cauldron (or mug) and top with your whip cream mixture.

4. Finish by sprinkling with butterscotch sweets then serve.

xxxxxxxxxxxxxxxxxxxxxxxxxxxxxxxxxxxxxxxxxx

Recipe 9 - The Ravenclaw House

This recipe shows you how to create the perfect Ravenclaw welcome drink.

Serving Size: 1

Preparation Time: 15 minutes

List of Ingredients:

- Vodka (1 oz., blueberry)
- Tonic Water (2 oz.)
- Blueberries (14, fresh

xxxxxxxxxxxxxxxxxxxxxxxxxxxxxxxxxxxxxxxxxx

Instructions:

1. Add all your ingredients to a shaker.

2. Shake well and serve.

xxxxxxxxxxxxxxxxxxxxxxxxxxxxxxxxxxxxxxxxxx

Recipe 10 - Knickerbocker Glory

Now you can enjoy this sweet treat that Dudley had in the Sorcerer's Stone.

Serving Size: 1

Preparation Time: 15 min

List of Ingredients:

- Chopped Fruit (1 cup, mix and match your favorite fruits)
- Ice Cream (3 scoops, vanilla)
- Fruit Syrup (3 tablespoons, peach)
- Clotted Cream (1 cup)
- Cherry (1)
- Ice Cream Wafer (1/4)
- Hazelnuts (1 tablespoon chopped)

xxxxxxxxxxxxxxxxxxxxxxxxxxxxxxxxxxxxxxxxx

Instructions:

1. In a tall milkshake glass add your chopped fruit.

2. Top your fruit with your ice cream.

3. Pour your fruit syrup over your ice cream.

4. Top with whipped cream and add in a wafer.

5. Finish with a cherry and hazelnuts.

xxxxxxxxxxxxxxxxxxxxxxxxxxxxxxxxxxxxxxxxx

Recipe 11 - The Slytherin House

This drink will fly you straight to the Slytherin House.

Serving Size: 1

Preparation Time: 5 min

List of Ingredients:

- Mint Leaves (4)
- Rum (1oz.)
- Lime Slices (2)
- Sugar (3 teaspoons)
- Champagne (3 oz.)

xxxxxxxxxxxxxxxxxxxxxxxxxxxxxxxxxxxxxxxxxx

Instructions:

1. Add all your ingredients to a shaker.

2. Shake well and serve.

xxxxxxxxxxxxxxxxxxxxxxxxxxxxxxxxxxxxxxxxxx

Recipe 12 - Bertie Bott's Jelly Beans

Who doesn't love Jelly Beans? Now you can enjoy the same unique flavors Harry, and his friends did.

Serving Size: 6

Preparation Time: 15 min

List of Ingredients:

- Water (3/4 cup)
- Sugar (1 ¼ cups)
- Gelatin (1/4 cup, powdered)
- Flavoring Agents and Colouring (6 different flavors, be sure to include some that are not so nice)
- Oil Spray (1 can)

Direction

1. Set your water on in a sauce pan over medium heat. Top with your sugar and allow to cook undisturbed until the sugar dissolves.

2. Add in your gelatin and cook until it reaches 110 degrees C (about 20 min)

3. Spray your jelly bean molds with oil spray then set up your flavor bowls.

4. Add some of your sugar mixture to each flavor then add in your color drops and stir well so that your color and flavor mix in well.

5. Pour the mixture into your jelly bean molds and allow the beans to dry overnight.

6. Enjoy!

xxxxxxxxxxxxxxxxxxxxxxxxxxxxxxxxxxxxxxxxxx

Recipe 13 - Gryffindor House

Here is a must have for the Gryffindor house occupants.

Serving Size: 1

Preparation Time: 10 minutes

List of Ingredients:

- Light Rum (1 oz.)
- Brandy (1/4 oz.)
- Lemon Juice (1/4 oz.)
- Raspberries (4)
- Raspberry Syrup (2 teaspoons)

XXXXXXXXXXXXXXXXXXXXXXXXXXXXXXXXXXXXXXXXX

Instructions:

1. Add all your ingredients to a shaker.

2. Shake well and serve.

XXXXXXXXXXXXXXXXXXXXXXXXXXXXXXXXXXXXXXXXX

Recipe 14 - Unicorn Blood Cocktail

Here is a magical cocktail that any Harry Potter fan can easily appreciate.

Serving Size: 4

Preparation Time: 30 min

List of Ingredients:

- Raspberry Puree (1 cups)
- Shimmery Liqueur (1 cup)
- Luster Dust (4 tablespoons, purple)
- Dry Ice (4 tablespoons)

XXXXXXXXXXXXXXXXXXXXXXXXXXXXXXXXXXXXXXXXXXXX

Instructions:

1. Dust 4 martini glasses lightly with luster dust (around the walls)

2. Fill the glasses 2/3 way up with raspberry puree, then evenly add your shimmery liqueur in the 4 glasses.

3. Add one tablespoon of Dry Ice to each drink and serve immediately.

XXXXXXXXXXXXXXXXXXXXXXXXXXXXXXXXXXXXXXXXXXXX

Recipe 15 - Butterbeer Ice Cream

This ice cream is just as delicious as the drink. Perfect on a hot summers day.

Serving Size: 8

Time: 40 minutes + inactive time

List of Ingredients:

- 1 cup butterbeer
- 1 cup heavy cream
- 2 cups half-and-half
- 6 egg yolks
- 1 tablespoon honey
- ½ cups caster sugar, divided
- Salt (1/2 teaspoons)

XXXXXXXXXXXXXXXXXXXXXXXXXXXXXXXXXXXXXXXXX

Instructions:

1. In a saucepan whisk the butterbeer, heavy cream, half-and-half, egg yolks and half of sugar.

2. Cook over medium-high heat, whisking for 12 minutes or until slightly thickened.

3. Pour the prepared mixture into a large bowl and chill for 2 hours.

4. Pour prepared egg yolk mixture into an ice cream maker machine and process according to manufacturer directions. Serve and enjoy.

NOTE: If you do not own the ice cream making a machine, cover the ice cream mix and freeze for 4-6 hours, stirring after each hour to prevent ice crystal formation.

xxxxxxxxxxxxxxxxxxxxxxxxxxxxxxxxxxxxxxxxxx

Recipe 16 - Polyjuice Potion

This sweet and spicy concoction is bound to knock you off your feet.

Serving Size: 3

Preparation Time: 15

List of Ingredients:

- Ginger Tea (3 tablespoons, sweetened)
- Orange Juice (1 cup, no pulp)
- Peach Slices (2, crushed)
- Sprite (1/2 cup)
- Food Coloring (1 drop, blue)
- Vodka (4 tablespoons)

XXXXXXXXXXXXXXXXXXXXXXXXXXXXXXXXXXXXXXXXXX

Instructions:

1. Mix all your ingredients together in a large bowl.

2. Adjust the color by adding more if desired.

3. Serve chilled.

XXXXXXXXXXXXXXXXXXXXXXXXXXXXXXXXXXXXXXXXXX

Recipe 17 - Avada Tequila

This spooky potion is perfect for a quick pick me up.

Serving Size: 1

Preparation Time: 5 minutes

List of Ingredients:

- Tequila (1/2 oz.)
- Absinthe (1/2 oz.)
- Mountain Dew (1/2 oz.)

xxxxxxxxxxxxxxxxxxxxxxxxxxxxxxxxxxxxxxxxxxxx

Instructions:

1. Add all your ingredients to a shot glass and serve.

xxxxxxxxxxxxxxxxxxxxxxxxxxxxxxxxxxxxxxxxxxxx

Recipe 18 - Goblet of Fire

Will you be the champion chosen to compete for this time around? Let consult the Goblet of Fire.

Serving Size:1

Preparation Time: 15 min

List of Ingredients:

- Vodka (1 oz.)
- Curacao (1 oz., blue)
- Lemonade (3 oz.)
- Rum (a splash)
- Cinnamon (a pinch)

xxxxxxxxxxxxxxxxxxxxxxxxxxxxxxxxxxxxxxxxxx

Instructions:

1. Combine the first 4 ingredients together thoroughly the pour in a wine glass.

2. Carefully set your drink on fire then sprinkle with cinnamon.

3. Serve!

xxxxxxxxxxxxxxxxxxxxxxxxxxxxxxxxxxxxxxxxxx

Recipe 19 - Confunda Chambardo

This drink is said to confuse your victims just like the Confundus Charm.

Serving Size: 1

Preparation Time: 15 minutes

List of Ingredients:

- Chambord (1/2oz.)
- Gin (1/2 oz.)
- Bacardi (1/8 oz.)
- Vanilla Coke (8 oz.)
- Ice (10 cubes)

xxxxxxxxxxxxxxxxxxxxxxxxxxxxxxxxxxxxxxxxxxx

Instructions:

1. Add all your ingredients to a tumbler.

2. Stir and serve.

xxxxxxxxxxxxxxxxxxxxxxxxxxxxxxxxxxxxxxxxxxx

Recipe 20 - The Albus Dumbledore

Here is a tasty drink inspired by Headmaster Dumbledore.

Serving Size: 1

Preparation Time: 15 min

List of Ingredients:

- Vodka (1 shot, lemon)
- Sprite (1 cup)
- Whipped Cream (1/2 cup, coconut, stiff)
- Lemon Zest (1 teaspoon)
- Ice (5 cubes)

Direction

1. Add your ice o your glass then pour in your vodka.

2. Top off with spite and finish with stiff whipped cream and lemon zest.

3. Enjoy!

xxxxxxxxxxxxxxxxxxxxxxxxxxxxxxxxxxxxxxxxxx

Recipe 21 - Chocolate Frog Jelly Shots

These chocolate frogs are to die for.

Serving Size: 18

Preparation Time: 15 minutes (plus setting time)

List of Ingredients:

- Water (1/2 cup)
- Gelatin Powder (2 envelopes)
- Ice Cream (3/8 cup, melted)
- Liqueur (1/2 cup, chocolate)
- Baileys (1/4 cup)
- Vodka (1/4 cup)
- Amaretto (1/8 cup)

XXXXXXXXXXXXXXXXXXXXXXXXXXXXXXXXXXXXXXXXXX

Instructions:

1. Set your water in a sauce pan over low heat and add in your gelatin powder.

2. Continue to stir until the gelatin is completely dissolved.

3. Spray your mold with oil spray and wipe away the excess with a hand towel.

4. Remove from heat and stir in your ice cream, liqueurs, and vodka.

5. Pour mixture into your frog molds and refrigerate until fully set.

6. Serve and enjoy!

xxxxxxxxxxxxxxxxxxxxxxxxxxxxxxxxxxxxxxxxx

Recipe 22 - Firewhiskey

This dish is not for the faint of heart as it literally feels like your mouth is on fire!

Serving Size: 1

Preparation Time: 15 min

List of Ingredients:

- Whiskey (1 oz.)
- Cinnamon Schnapps (1/2 oz.)
- Rum (1 tablespoon)

xxxxxxxxxxxxxxxxxxxxxxxxxxxxxxxxxxxxxxxxxx

Instructions:

1. Add in your cinnamon schnapps and whisking into a shaker with ice.

2. Shake well and pour into a shot glass.

73. Top with rum and carefully set the drink on fire.

4. Serve and enjoy!

xxxxxxxxxxxxxxxxxxxxxxxxxxxxxxxxxxxxxxxxxx

Recipe 23 - Butterbeer Jelly Shots

Now you can turn the most popular drink from Harry Potter into jelly shots

Serving Size: 18

Preparation Time: 15 minutes (plus setting time)

List of Ingredients:

- Butterbeer (2 cups)
- Gelatin Powder (3 envelopes, plain)
- Vodka (1 cup, pineapple or ginger)

xxxxxxxxxxxxxxxxxxxxxxxxxxxxxxxxxxxxxxxxx

Instructions:

1. Set your Butterbeer in a sauce pan over low heat and add in your gelatin powder.

2. Continue to stir until the gelatin is completely dissolved.

3. Remove from heat and stir in your vodka.

4. Refrigerate until fully set.

5. Cut into rectangles and serve!

xxxxxxxxxxxxxxxxxxxxxxxxxxxxxxxxxxxxxxxxx

Recipe 24 - Pureblood

This drink will let you see if you are as pure as your bloodline.

Serving Size: 1

Preparation Time: 15 min

List of Ingredients:

- Vodka (2½ oz.)
- Sweet & Sour Mix (4 oz.)
- Raspberry Liqueur (1 oz.)
- Raspberry (4, to garnish)

xxxxxxxxxxxxxxxxxxxxxxxxxxxxxxxxxxxxxxxxx

Instructions:

1. Add your 3 first ingredients with ice in a shaker.

2. Shake well and pour into a shot glass.

3. Garnish with raspberry and serve!

xxxxxxxxxxxxxxxxxxxxxxxxxxxxxxxxxxxxxxxxx

Recipe 25 - Pumkintini

This pumpkin cocktail is delicious and is bound to have you feeling like a wizard.

Serving Size: 2

Preparation Time: 15 min

List of Ingredients:

- Graham Crackers (2, crushed)
- Ice (12)
- White Rum (6 tablespoons)
- Pumpkin (6 tablespoons, pureed)
- Maple Syrup (1½ tablespoon)
- Whiskey (1/2 tablespoons)
- Cinnamon (1 teaspoon)
- Cloves (1 teaspoon)
- Ginger (1 teaspoon, ground)
- Coconut Milk (2 tablespoons)

xxxxxxxxxxxxxxxxxxxxxxxxxxxxxxxxxxxxxxxxxx

Instructions:

1. Add all your ingredients, except for graham crackers, to a shaker and shake well.

2. Wet the edges of 2 martini glasses and place the rim into your graham cracker crumbs.

3. Strain the mixture into the glass and serve.

xxxxxxxxxxxxxxxxxxxxxxxxxxxxxxxxxxxxxxxxxx

Recipe 26 - The Phoenix Feather

If the basilisk of life nips you with its fangs, you will need this drink to help you fight back.

Serving Size: 1

Preparation Time: 15 min

List of Ingredients:

- Lillet Blanc (2 oz.)
- Campari (1.5 oz.)
- Grapefruit Juice (1 oz.)
- Club Soda (1 cup)

xxxxxxxxxxxxxxxxxxxxxxxxxxxxxxxxxxxxxxxxx

Instructions:

1. Add your first 3 ingredients with ice into a shaker.

2. Shake well and pour your juice into a tall glass.

3. Top up with club soda and serve.

xxxxxxxxxxxxxxxxxxxxxxxxxxxxxxxxxxxxxxxxx

Recipe 27 - Polyjuice Potion Jelly Shots

Delicious Harry Potter inspired Jello Shots made with Polyjuice Potion.

Serving Size: 18

Preparation Time: 15 minutes (plus setting time)

List of Ingredients:

- Polyjuice Potion (2 cups)
- Gelatin Powder (3 envelopes, plain)
- Vodka (1 cup, pineapple or ginger)

xxxxxxxxxxxxxxxxxxxxxxxxxxxxxxxxxxxxxxxx

Instructions:

1. Set your Polyjuice Potion in a sauce pan over low heat and add in your gelatin powder.

2. Continue to stir until the gelatin is completely dissolved.

3. Remove from heat and stir in your vodka.

4. Refrigerate until fully set.

5. Cut into rectangles and serve!

xxxxxxxxxxxxxxxxxxxxxxxxxxxxxxxxxxxxxxxx

Recipe 28 - Liquid Luck

Liquid Luck, also known as the Felix Felicis is said to improve your luck.

Serving Size: 1

Preparation Time: 15 min

List of Ingredients:

- Simple Syrup (1/4 oz.)
- Lemon Juice (1/4 oz.)
- Ginger Beer (1.5 oz.)
- Champagne (1 cup)

XXXXXXXXXXXXXXXXXXXXXXXXXXXXXXXXXXXXXXXX

Instructions:

1. In a champagne flute mix together your lemon juice and simple syrup.

2. Add in your ginger beer then top off with champagne.

3. Serve and enjoy!

XXXXXXXXXXXXXXXXXXXXXXXXXXXXXXXXXXXXXXXX

Recipe 29 - The Severus Snape

Here is a cocktail that pays homage to Professor Snape.

Serving Size: 1

Preparation Time: 15 minutes

List of Ingredients:

- Amaretto (1oz shot)
- Doctor Pepper (1 cup)
- Ice (1/4 cup)

xxxxxxxxxxxxxxxxxxxxxxxxxxxxxxxxxxxxxxxxxx

Instructions:

1. Add your ice to a cocktail glass then proceed to pour in your Amaretto.

2. Top off the glass with Doctor Pepper.

3. Stir and serve.

xxxxxxxxxxxxxxxxxxxxxxxxxxxxxxxxxxxxxxxxxx

Recipe 30 - Amortentia – The Love Potion

This recipe is said to be able to help you get your love to fall for you.

Serving Size: 1

Preparation Time: 15 min (plus time to make ice ring)

List of Ingredients:

Ice Ring

- Red Raspberries (1 pint, fresh)
- Pomegranate Seeds (1 cup, fresh)
- Water (4 cups, boiled)
- Ice Cubes (2 trays)

Punch

- Aperol (750ml)
- Pomegranate Juice (4 cups)
- Gin (2 cups)
- Rose (1500 ml, chilled)

xxxxxxxxxxxxxxxxxxxxxxxxxxxxxxxxxxxxxxxxxxx

Instructions:

1. Evenly spread your seeds in the bottom of a Bundt cake pan and proceed to cover the seeds with your fruits and ice.

2. Pour your boiling water over the ice and allow to freeze overnight.

3. Combine all your juice ingredients into a large bowl and mix well.

4. Serve in a cocktail glass with your ice ring floating on top.

XXXXXXXXXXXXXXXXXXXXXXXXXXXXXXXXXXXXXXXXX

Made in the USA
Monee, IL
13 December 2019

18627106R00042